"The water was choppy, the deck awash with vomit." That's how one young U.S. soldier, Benjamin Alvarado, described his trip across the English Channel on June 6, 1944—D-Day.

He was one of 170,000 Allied troops headed for Normandy, France. They were part of a massive invasion force whose mission was to free Europe from the brutal German dictator, Adolf Hitler. "I was numb with fear of what I was about to encounter," Alvarado recalled.

He had good reason to be afraid.

A U.S. soldier lies in the surf on Omaha
Beach, Normandy, pinned down by German
machine-gun fire.

The slaughter began the moment Private Alvarado landed on the beach.

"Shells [were] bursting around us, bullets whizzing by," he recalled. "At the water's edge, I tripped over several dead GIs. . . . Bodies were everywhere!"

The surf was running red with blood. And D-Day had just begun.

Photographs © 2010: **Airborne & Special Operations Museum/spec 56/06jpg:** 39 top; **akg-Images, London:** 23 top; **Alamy Images/Interfoto:** 25 top left; **AP Images:** 30 (Army Signal Corps), back cover, 57 top (Peter J. Carroll), 37 (Pool), cover (U.S. Coast Guard, hand-tinted by Red Herring Design), 28, 29 (U.S. Signal Corps), 12, 35 top, 38, 47, 48, 51, 55 bottom; **Corbis Images:** 7 top, 9 top, 10 top, 18 top, 22 bottom, 23 bottom, 33, 52 (Bettmann), 10 bottom, 11 bottom (Hulton Archive), 8 foreground (Hulton-Deutsch Collection), 35 bottom (Ted Streshinsky), 8 background; **Courtesy of David Allender, WarChronicle.com:** 53, 54, 55 top; **Getty Images:** 13 (AFP), 44 top (Morris Engel), 9 bottom (Fox Photos), 46 (Cynthia Johnson/Time & Life Pictures), 24 (Keystone), 21 bottom (New York Times Co.), 16, 17 (Popperfoto), 39 bottom, 40 top (Fred Ramage/Keystone), 21 top, 41 (Frank Scherschel), 7 bottom, 34 (The Frank S. Errigo Archive), 22 top (US Air Force); **Courtesy of the Hershey-Derry Township Historical Society:** 31; **Library of Congress:** 26, 27 left; **Magnum Photos/Robert Capa/© 2001 Cornell Capa:** 2, 3, 45, 49; **National Archives and Records Administration:** 56 (ARC 111-SC-190120), 32 (ARC 111-SC-354702), 5 (ARC 195515), 57 bottom (ARC 208-AA-206K-31), 40 bottom (ARC 242-GAP-286B-4), 42, 43 (ARC 531187), 11 top (ARC 86-WWT-3-67), 44 bottom (ARC N.d. 26-G-2624); **National Museum of American History, Smithsonian Institution:** 25 top right (Neg# 2004-25307.09), 25 bottom left (Hugh Talman/Neg# 2004-29586.15), 25 bottom right (Hugh Talman/Neg# 2004-49440); **The Art Archive/Picture Desk/National Archives, Washington DC:** 1; The Granger Collection, New York/ullstein bild: 18 bottom, 19; **The Image Works:** 27 right (Public Record Office/HIP), 14, 15 (Topham).

Maps by David Lindroth, Inc.

CONTENT CONSULTANT: Kenneth Hoffman, Director of Education, The National World War II Museum, New Orleans

Book design: Red Herring Design/NYC

Library of Congress Cataloging-in-Publication Data
D-Day : the Allies strike back during World War II / Terry Miller.
p. cm. - (24/7: goes to war)
Includes bibliographical references and index.
ISBN-13: 978-0-531-25527-8 (lib. bdg.)   978-0-531-25452-3 (pbk.)
ISBN-10: 0-531-25527-1 (lib. bdg.)   0-531-25452-6 (pbk.)
1. World War, 1939–1945—Campaigns—France—Normandy—
Juvenile literature. I. Title
D756.5.N6M493 2010
940.54'21421—dc22   2009016544

1 2 3 4 5 6 7 8 9 10 R 19 18 17 16 15 14 13 12 11 10 09

D-DAY

The Allies Strike Back During World War II

TERRY MILLER

Franklin Watts®
An Imprint of Scholastic Inc.

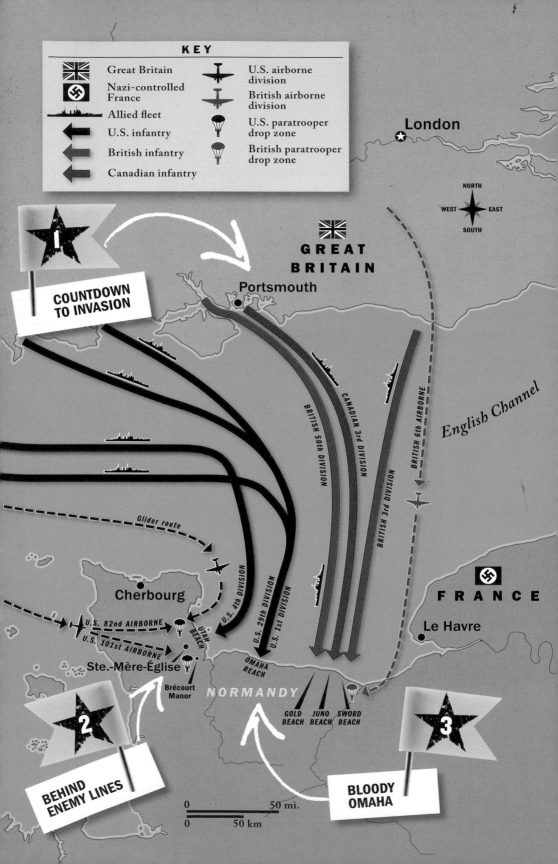

KEY

	Great Britain		U.S. airborne division
	Nazi-controlled France		British airborne division
	Allied fleet		U.S. paratrooper drop zone
	U.S. infantry		British paratrooper drop zone
	British infantry		
	Canadian infantry		

London

1

COUNTDOWN TO INVASION

GREAT BRITAIN

Portsmouth

NORTH
WEST — EAST
SOUTH

English Channel

BRITISH 50th DIVISION

CANADIAN 3rd DIVISION

BRITISH 3rd DIVISION

BRITISH 6th AIRBORNE

Glider route

U.S. 4th DIVISION

Cherbourg

U.S. 82nd AIRBORNE

UTAH BEACH

U.S. 101st AIRBORNE

Ste.-Mère-Église

Brécourt Manor

2

BEHIND ENEMY LINES

U.S. 29th DIVISION

U.S. 1st DIVISION

OMAHA BEACH

NORMANDY

FRANCE

Le Havre

GOLD BEACH

JUNO BEACH

SWORD BEACH

3

BLOODY OMAHA

0	50 mi.
0	50 km

CONTENTS

D-DAY
June 6, 1944

On D-Day, more than 170,000 Allied troops crossed the English Channel and landed in Normandy, France. Most of the soldiers were from Canada, Great Britain, and the United States. The troops were the first wave of a massive operation to liberate Europe from German occupation.

over•

DARKNESS
FALLS ON
EUROPE

German dictator Adolf Hitler (left). German tanks, or *panzers*, on parade in Poland after Hitler's army invaded the country in 1939 (above).

I t was known as "lightning war," *blitzkrieg* in German, and the people of Poland were the first to feel its effects.

On September 1, 1939, thousands of German warplanes swarmed over Poland. They blasted the Polish air force out of the sky and demolished Poland's rail lines. Then more than a million German troops raced into Poland.

The relentless assault quickly erased an entire nation from the map. Poland was divided between Germany and Germany's ally, the Soviet Union.

World War II had begun.

Led by Adolf Hitler, Germany posed a grave threat to the world. Since seizing power in 1933, Hitler's Nazi Party had abolished democracy and built up a huge army. Political opponents, Jews, and other groups considered "inferior" by the Nazis had been stripped of their rights and thrown into concentration camps.

Jews in the Netherlands (shown here) and other German-occupied countries were forced to wear yellow stars.

Now, with his *panzer* tanks poised on the French border, Hitler stood ready to conquer the rest of Europe. On May 10, 1940, German troops flooded into Belgium, Luxembourg, and the Netherlands. A few weeks later, France fell to the Nazis. It was "the most famous victory in history," Hitler crowed.

A building in London damaged by German bombs

After the fall of France, Britain stood alone against the Nazi threat. As German planes dropped bombs on British cities, Prime Minister Winston Churchill vowed to fight with "blood, toil, tears, and sweat" until Hitler fell. "If we fail," he warned, "then the whole world, including the United States . . . will sink into the abyss of a new Dark Age."

For two years, U.S. President Franklin D. Roosevelt steered the United States clear of the war in Europe.

Ships at Pearl Harbor burn after being hit by Japanese bombs and torpedoes.

But by the end of 1941, Hitler was more threatening than ever. He had drawn Japan and Italy into a powerful alliance known as the Axis. He had invaded his former ally the Soviet Union (the USSR). His bombers continued to attack British cities. And his U-boat submarines sank U.S. ships that carried much-needed supplies to Britain. The Allies—Britain, the USSR, and other countries—desperately needed help.

America at War

But it was Japan—not Germany—that forced the U.S. into action. On December 7, 1941, Japanese planes attacked and crippled the U.S. Pacific Fleet at Pearl Harbor, Hawaii. Declaring it a "day that will live in infamy," Roosevelt threw the United States into the war, joining the Allies.

Americans mobilized on all fronts. Auto plants churned out tanks, planes, and guns for the military. Families scrounged scrap metal and rubber tires to supply weapons factories. Two million women went to work on assembly lines.

For several months, however, nothing could stop the Axis powers. The Japanese navy swept through the Pacific, seizing Guam, the Philippines,

With U.S. men fighting overseas, the number of women in the labor force increased by more than 50 percent during the war. Here, a worker pauses in an airplane factory in 1942.

and Malaya. At the same time, German armies continued to press hard in the USSR and North Africa.

The Allied leaders—Roosevelt, Churchill, and Soviet Premier Josef Stalin—agreed on a strategy. They would try to hold off the Japanese in the Pacific. But their first goal would be to defeat Hitler.

Stalin wanted the U.S. and Britain to invade Europe as soon as possible. But Churchill and Roosevelt decided to sweep Hitler out of Africa first. In November 1942, Allied troops stormed ashore in North Africa.

Leaders of the "Big Three" Allies in 1945. Left to right: Winston Churchill (Britain); Franklin D. Roosevelt (U.S.); and Josef Stalin (USSR).

11

British soldiers run for cover in North Africa in 1943.

In early 1943, U.S. and British tanks rolled through the North African desert, trapping German Field Marshal Erwin Rommel—the crafty "Desert Fox"—in Tunisia. Hitler ordered his troops to fight "to the last bullet." But by May, the exhausted Axis commanders gave in, handing over 250,000 prisoners and control of the North African coast.

Now the Allies controlled the Mediterranean Sea. Across it lay the southern coast of Nazi-occupied Europe.

In July 1943, half a million Allied soldiers crossed the

In the spring of 1944, most of Europe was under the control of Nazi Germany. Its leader, Adolf Hitler, hoped to add Britain and the USSR to his conquests.

Jewish prisoners in Poland in 1943. The Nazis set up five concentration camps in Poland; most of the country's Jews were killed.

Mediterranean and landed in Sicily. As the troops advanced through Sicily, the Italian people overthrew their dictator, Benito Mussolini, and signed a truce with the Allies. After four years of war, the Allies had regained a foothold in Europe.

But Hitler clung fiercely to the rest of Europe. In northern Italy, German troops fought the Allies to a standstill. On the Eastern Front, the Soviet army lost millions of soldiers as they tried to push the Germans out of the USSR.

Operation Overlord

Grim reports from Germany gave the Allied task new urgency. Millions of people, many of them Jews, were imprisoned in concentration camps in Germany and Eastern Europe. There, Hitler was carrying out the Final Solution, a plan to murder every Jew in Europe. With the clock ticking, Churchill and Roosevelt approved Operation Overlord, the plan for an Allied invasion of northern France. The start date was known as D-Day.

If Overlord succeeded, Hitler would be trapped between the invasion force advancing from the west and the Soviet army in the east. If the operation failed, it would be years before the Allies could gather the strength to try again.

The countdown to D-Day had begun.

★ COUNTDOWN TO INV

Adolf Hitler's armies had occupied most of Europe. Could Allied forces invade the continent and liberate millions of people living under Nazi rule?

ASION

British troops train for the D-Day invasion by storming a beach in Devon, England.

Dwight D. Eisenhower stepped out of his car into the driving rain. It was 4 A.M. on June 5, 1944. The U.S. general had just arrived at a mansion called Southwick House, near the town of Portsmouth, England. Inside, waiting for him, were the commanders of the American and British armies.

As supreme commander of the Allied Expeditionary Force (AEF), Eisenhower was in charge of armed forces from the United States, Britain, Canada, and other countries that had united to invade Europe and defeat Adolf Hitler of Germany.

Eisenhower hurried into the mansion. He entered the living room, where the officers were gathered around a fireplace, drinking coffee. They bolted to their feet and saluted.

Each man knew that Eisenhower was about to make a decision that would determine the outcome of the war.

General Dwight D. Eisenhower (center) and his top U.S. and British commanders in February 1944

Supreme Commander Dwight Eisenhower (with foot on platform) watches Allied troops as they train for the invasion of Normandy.

About 170,000 soldiers were assembled nearby, waiting to take part in the largest seaborne invasion ever. A massive fleet would carry them across the stormy English Channel to France. They'd be the first wave of a military campaign made up of about three million soldiers. The goal of the mission: to free Europe's 300 million people from Adolf Hitler's savage grip.

But before Eisenhower could launch the invasion, he had to get a final weather report. The day before, he had learned that a fierce storm was on its way. He had postponed the invasion for 24 hours. Now, huddled around the fireplace with his generals, Eisenhower was told that the storm could die down for about 36 hours. He had a small window in which to launch the attack.

He mulled over his options. So far, the Allies had managed to keep Hitler in the dark about the invasion. Another delay would give the Nazis more time to discover where and when it would take place. Then again: what if Eisenhower okayed the invasion and the storm didn't break? Rough seas could doom the whole operation before any troops ever landed in France.

The fate of his troops—and millions of other people—hung on his decision.

Storming Fortress Europe

Five months earlier, Eisenhower had been given the toughest military assignment in history.

President Franklin Roosevelt had ordered him to "enter the continent of Europe and . . . undertake operations aimed at the heart of Germany and the destruction of her armed forces."

Hitler's seven million troops had a stranglehold on Europe. The continent was so heavily defended that the Germans called it "Festung Europa"— Fortress Europe.

Hitler had ordered artillery bunkers like this one to be built along the western coast of Europe.

The invasion—codenamed Overlord—would be the most complex military operation in history. And until recently, few would have guessed that Roosevelt would choose Eisenhower— or "Ike," as he was nicknamed—to command it.

As a young man, Ike hadn't seemed destined for greatness. Out of the 164 students in his class at the U.S. Military Academy at West Point, Ike ranked 125th in discipline. True, since then he had led victorious campaigns in North Africa and Italy. But he didn't have a tough image. He was known more for his friendly grin and his skill in working with rival generals.

He would need that team-building talent now. The troops under his command included 1.7 million Americans, one million British and Canadian soldiers, and about 300,000 soldiers from France, Poland, Norway, and other European countries.

It was an enormous job. But Eisenhower was a confident and optimistic man. In January 1944, he flew to England and got to work.

German Field Marshal Erwin Rommel (holding stick) inspects beach defenses in France at low tide. These tripods were designed to rip open any Allied ships that tried to land at high tide.

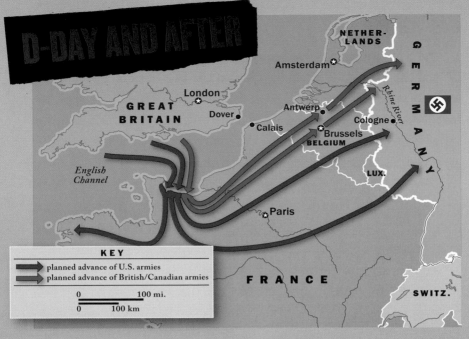

D-DAY AND AFTER

D-Day was just the first step in the Allied plan for invading Western Europe. First, troops would land in Normandy, in northern France. Then, millions of U.S., British, and other Allied troops would sweep across France and into Germany.

"Not Enough Wallop"

Where would the invasion take place?

Ike okayed the choice of Normandy, a province in France. It wasn't an obvious pick. Normandy was 100 miles south of England. There were many closer sites. But Ike and the other planners reasoned that Hitler would never expect the Allies to land at Normandy.

"The element of surprise," Ike said, "would be our greatest advantage."

The invasion was planned for May 1, 1944—or "D-Day." That's the military term for the start date of any major operation. Ike now had fewer than four months to finish assembling and training the army.

His next job was to beef up the invasion force. The original Overlord plan didn't have "enough wallop in [it]," he said.

Eisenhower wanted more weapons and more vehicles. He

arranged to have half a million tons of guns, tanks, and planes shipped from the U.S. to England every month.

He also needed more troops. When Ike took command of Overlord, there were about 100,000 American soldiers in England. That wasn't nearly enough. Under his orders, 1.6 million more American fighting men hurried to England, joining the other Allied troops who

A U.S. soldier stacks cans of gasoline in preparation for the D-Day invasion.

were gathering there. By D-Day, one out of every 27 people in England was an American.

The training was intense. Infantrymen practiced storming beaches that resembled those in Normandy. Paratroopers rehearsed jumping from planes at night and locating targets in the dark. At the same time, Allied planes flew bombing raids into France, destroying the ports, roads, and railroads the Germans used to move supplies to their troops.

As May 1 approached, Eisenhower decided that his troops still needed more training and supplies. Reluctantly, he delayed the invasion date to early June.

P-47 Thunderbolt fighter planes from the U.S. lined up on an airfield in Britain

In the weeks before D-Day, U.S. planes dropped thousands of bombs on German defenses in Normandy.

Fooling Hitler

The Germans knew that an invasion was coming.

That spring, Hitler had warned his generals that the Allies would launch an attack. But "how and where it will come, no one knows," he said.

To keep Hitler guessing, the Allies came up with an elaborate deception. Operation Fortitude was designed to convince the Germans that the Allies would strike near the French port of Calais. It was a logical site for the invasion. Calais is much closer to England than Normandy is—it's only 25 miles from the nearest English town, Dover.

With the help of a movie company,

the Allies created the illusion that there was an entire army based in Dover. They built thousands of fake tanks, airplanes, and landing craft—and placed the props where German planes were sure to spot them. They blasted sound effects of marching boots and shouting officers through loudspeakers in the town.

To complete the deception, the Allies even transmitted phony radio messages about troops preparing to land in Calais. The messages were sure to be intercepted by German spies.

Operation Fortitude worked perfectly. One of Hitler's top generals, Erwin Rommel, sent 200,000 soldiers to protect the Calais region. He didn't leave Normandy undefended, but when the Allies landed there, many of his best troops were 150 miles from the fighting.

German gunners in a bunker on the coast

Many years later, an interviewer asked Eisenhower about Operation Fortitude. Ike laughed and said, "By God, we fooled them, didn't we?"

"Okay, We'll Go"

By April, Britain was packed with soldiers, tanks, and planes.

People joked that the island might sink under the weight of so much equipment.

In late May, the soldiers suddenly vanished from their camps. Their training grounds were empty. The village pubs were quiet again.

Eisenhower had given the order: Move the troops to Britain's southern

From the air, this phony, inflatable tank looked like the real thing.

British Royal Marines train for the D-Day invasion in early 1944.

coast. The invasion was about to begin. About 170,000 men—the first soldiers who would land in Normandy—jammed into the harbor areas. It took 4,500 cooks just to prepare their meals.

The soldiers received detailed instructions about their missions. Up until then, they'd been kept in the dark about where the invasion would take place. Now, they pored over maps of Normandy. The men were confined to camp so they wouldn't leak the top-secret plans. They weren't even allowed to write home.

On May 31, soldiers began boarding the transport ships that would take them to France. Some men couldn't wait to fight the Nazis. Others griped about the cramped quarters. Still others prayed or nervously checked their weapons. Many fell seasick as violent winds and waves rocked the ships.

The fleet left port on June 3, but the ships were called back when bad weather forced Eisenhower to delay the invasion. In the early hours of June 5, as Eisenhower met with his generals at Southwick House, the ships were back in port, still crammed with soldiers.

THE THINGS THEY CARRIED

The troops who landed on Normandy's beaches had to fight through deadly enemy defenses. Here are some of the weapons the Allied troops carried.

M1 SEMI-AUTOMATIC RIFLE: The standard infantry weapon, it was reliable and powerful and could be fired much more rapidly than German rifles.

MORTAR: This portable cannon fired explosive shells high into the air. The most powerful mortar shells could kill everyone within 60 feet of where they landed.

M1 BAZOOKA: This launcher fired a rocket that could pierce four inches of armor.

FLAMETHROWER: This fearsome weapon could shoot flaming gasoline up to 50 yards. Flamethrowers were used to burn German soldiers out of their fortifications. A soldier carrying a flamethrower was a prime target for the enemy.

That morning, Eisenhower listened to the weatherman's forecast: the storm *might* let up 36 hours. The fate of Overlord hinged on a tiny window of fair weather.

Ike asked his generals for their opinions, but they were divided over whether to launch the invasion. It was up to him. "The temptation to postpone is so great," he admitted.

Eisenhower thought silently for a minute. Then, shortly after 4:00 A.M., he stood up and gave the order.

"Okay," he said, "we'll go."

"Look Out, Hitler, Here We Come!"
By late afternoon on June 5, the fleet was underway.

More than 5,000 ships steamed across the English Channel toward Normandy. Crews readied the planes that would carry the 18,000 U.S. and British paratroopers who would jump into enemy territory shortly after midnight. Bombers took off, on their way to knock out the German defenses along the beaches.

Ike drank pots of black coffee and smoked nervously. Any number of things could go wrong, but there was no turning back now.

He spent that evening with the men of the 101st Airborne Division. As the paratroopers prepared for the flight, Eisenhower strolled among them. He thanked them and wished them luck. "Where are you from, soldier?" he asked over and over. He always hoped to find a man from his hometown of Abilene, Kansas.

Each paratrooper was weighed down with up to 200 pounds of equipment. But Eisenhower's presence seemed to lighten the men's load. One small paratrooper, whom Ike later described as "more equipment than soldier," saluted the general. When Eisenhower returned the salute, the soldier shouted, "Look out, Hitler, here we come!"

Finally, the men boarded their aircraft. The planes lifted off. They filled the skies over Eisenhower's head with a deafening roar.

Ike watched until the last plane flew out of sight. "Well—it's on," he said quietly. There were tears in his eyes.

General Eisenhower speaks with paratroopers before they take off for Normandy. Some have blackened their faces as nighttime camouflage.

Every soldier headed to Normandy received this letter from Eisenhower.

Soldiers, Sailors and Airmen of the Allied Expeditionary Force!

You are about to embark upon the Great Crusade, toward which we have striven these many months. The eyes of the world are upon you. The hopes and prayers of liberty-loving people everywhere march with you. In company with our brave Allies and brothers-in-arms on other Fronts, you will bring about the destruction of the German war machine, the elimination of Nazi tyranny over the oppressed peoples of Europe, and security for ourselves in a free world.

Your task will not be an easy one. Your enemy is well trained, well equipped and battle-hardened. He will fight savagely.

But this is the year 1944 ! Much has happened since the Nazi triumphs of 1940-41. The United Nations have inflicted upon the Germans great defeats, in open battle, man-to-man. Our air offensive has seriously reduced their strength in the air and their capacity to wage war on the ground. Our Home Fronts have given us an overwhelming superiority in weapons and munitions of war, and placed at our disposal great reserves of trained fighting men. The tide has turned ! The free men of the world are marching together to Victory !

I have full confidence in your courage, devotion to duty and skill in battle. We will accept nothing less than full Victory !

Good Luck ! And let us all beseech the blessing of Almighty God upon this great and noble undertaking.

Dwight D Eisenhower

27

2

U.S. paratroopers on their way to France. The men had trained long and hard for this mission.

BEHIND ENEMY LINES

Lieutenant Dick Winters had never been in combat before. But on D-Day, he would jump into enemy territory and lead a squad of paratroopers on a daring assault.

Paratroopers nearing their drop zone in Normandy wait for the green light—the signal to jump.

Lieutenant Dick Winters stood at the open door of his plane, feeling the night air rush in. The sky around him was thick with hundreds of aircraft, all flying in formation over the English Channel.

The planes were carrying 13,000 U.S. paratroopers from the 82nd and 101st Airborne divisions. They were headed toward Nazi-occupied France.

Winters was the leader of a platoon of 32 men in Easy Company, part of the 101st. Up to now, he hadn't seen any combat. But tonight, Easy Company would take part in an elaborate operation to wipe out German defenses before Allied soldiers stormed the beaches of Normandy at dawn.

Along with the rest of the 101st, Winters and his men were headed for drop zones near a stretch of Normandy coastline codenamed Utah Beach.

The mission of the 101st was to take out German troops defending the four exit roads from the beach. The roads were the only way for the invading Allies to move inland. The paratroopers also had to capture any German guns aimed at the roads.

If the 101st failed, the troops landing on the beach at dawn could be slaughtered. The landing force, Winters wrote later, was "counting on us to pave the way."

Now, as the planes neared the French coast, Winters glanced at his men. They had trained together for two years and were a tight-knit unit. Usually the guys passed the time joking around with each other. But tonight they sat quietly, lost in thought.

The red light came on. It was the signal to get ready. In a few minutes the light would turn green. And then they would jump.

1:10 A.M.: Under Attack

Suddenly, Winters's plane began to rock wildly. Anti-aircraft shells were exploding all around it.

The planes had just passed over the Normandy coast. Many pilots had dipped under the clouds to look for landmarks. At such a low altitude, they were easy targets for German gunners on the ground below.

Searchlights and tracer bullets lit up the night sky. Pilots broke out of formation and veered far off course. All around him, Winters saw planes on fire. His commander's plane plunged to earth and exploded. Then Winters felt his plane take a hit.

The green light came on. Winters and his men hadn't reached the drop zone yet, and their plane was flying too fast and too low. But it was safer to jump than to stay on the plane.

"Let's go!" Winters yelled to his men. Then he jumped.

1:20 A.M.: Behind Enemy Lines
Winters's parachute snapped open with a jolt.

The prop blast—the whoosh of air from the plane's propellers—sent Winters's equipment bag flying. Inside it were his rifle, grenades, and gear.

Bullets whizzed past. A machine gun was blasting away at him as he dropped toward the dark fields below.

He hit the ground—hard. He'd be black and blue for days.

But that was the least of his problems. The only weapon he had now was a knife. He couldn't see any of his men. And he was lost.

According to the plan, as soon as the men in Easy Company landed, they were supposed to go to previously assigned meeting points. Then they would make their way to a village called Ste.-Marie-du-Mont. There, they'd take out a garrison of German soldiers that was guarding one of the exit roads from Utah Beach—Exit 2.

In the pre-dawn hours of D-Day, thousands of U.S. and British paratroopers landed in Normandy. No photos of the jump are known to exist. This photo shows Allied paratroopers jumping into the Netherlands in late 1944.

Paratroopers in the 101st Airborne were loaded down with equipment. Each man carried up to 200 pounds of weapons, ammo, and food, as well as personal stuff like journals, letters, books, and cards.

M1 HELMET: This steel helmet could deflect flying shrapnel but not bullets.

.45-CALIBER PISTOL: Standard equipment for officers; most privates also carried one.

WATER CANTEEN: Troopers also carried tablets for purifying water.

M1 RIFLE: The standard gun for most troops.

PARACHUTES: Each trooper had a main parachute on his back plus an extra chute in a bag on his chest.

FIRST AID KIT: It contained bandages, painkillers, and antibiotics.

FOLDING SHOVEL: Used for digging protective foxholes.

EXPLOSIVES: The men carried plastic explosives, plus fuses, blasting caps, and detonators; one or more anti-tank mines; hand grenades; and smoke grenades.

A LOT OF BAGGAGE

Troopers stuffed their pockets with lots of gear, including a spoon, razor, flashlight, compass, socks, cigarettes, matches, $25 worth of French money, rations for three days, an emergency food package (containing chocolate, candy, powdered coffee, and sugar), ammo, and maps. They also carried a gas mask in case of chemical attacks, and a life jacket to keep them afloat in water.

THREE KNIVES: One was a trench knife, used in hand-to-hand combat. It had edges for both stabbing and slashing.

A paratrooper stands guard as other troopers gather up their parachutes during a training exercise in 1942.

But tonight, everything had gone wrong. The planes had veered out of formation to avoid anti-aircraft fire, forcing the men to jump too early. They had landed far from their drop zones.

Now, lost in the darkness, it was nearly impossible for the paratroopers to find each other—or their meeting points.

Still, for some reason, Winters wasn't scared. "Don't ask me why," he later wrote. Instead, "the long months of training kicked in." He grabbed his knife and set out to find his men.

2:00 A.M.: *Click-Clack, Click-Clack*

Winters hadn't gone very far before he spotted some people ahead. It was too dark to tell who they were.

He hid and pulled out his cricket—a small clicker. He clicked it once: *click-clack*. All the paratroopers had crickets so they could identify each other in the dark. If Winters didn't get two answering clicks, he'd assume the soldiers were German. But he heard the response he was hoping for: *click-clack, click-clack*.

Five men stepped forward, all from Easy Company.

One of them told Winters that he'd just seen a road sign for Ste.-Mère-Église. That clue helped. Winters realized that they were about five miles west

U.S. paratroopers hike along a road in Normandy two days after D-Day.

of their objective, Ste.-Marie-du-Mont. They had to get there by dawn to secure Exit Road No. 2 before the troops landed.

The group started walking east. They hoped to link up with other men from Easy Company along the way. They knew they couldn't take out a garrison of German soldiers by themselves.

6:00 A.M.: New Orders

Throughout the night, Winters heard shooting and artillery fire.

Paratroopers were skirmishing with soldiers from the large German force defending Normandy.

Winters's small band kept

A model of Private John Steele, a U.S. paratrooper who got caught on this church steeple in Ste.-Mère-Église moving toward Ste.-Marie-du-Mont. By 6:00 A.M., Winters had linked up with only 12 other men from Easy Company. For safety, he and his men had fallen in with a column of about 100 paratroopers from other companies.

About a mile outside of Ste.-Marie-du-Mont, the group stopped to rest in a small village where the 101st had set up a temporary command post. The paratroopers had just sat down to grab some food when Winters was summoned to meet with a senior officer.

Easy Company has a new assignment, the officer told Winters. Nearby, in a field next to a farmhouse called Brécourt Manor, four German cannons had started blasting away at U.S. troops landing on Utah Beach. It was up to Easy Company to

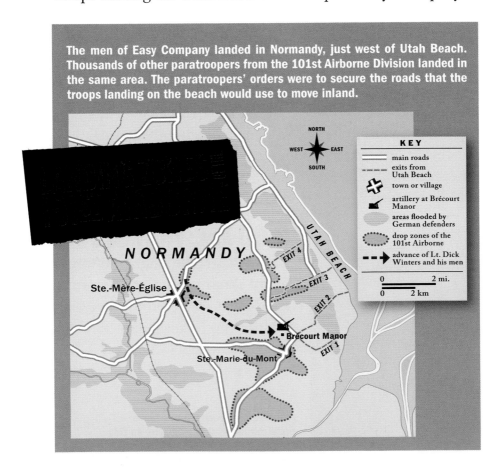

The men of Easy Company landed in Normandy, just west of Utah Beach. Thousands of other paratroopers from the 101st Airborne Division landed in the same area. The paratroopers' orders were to secure the roads that the troops landing on the beach would use to move inland.

U.S. paratroopers in Ste.-Mère-Église. They captured the town in the early hours of D-Day. It was the first town in France to be liberated by the Allies.

take the cannons out. And since his commander had been killed, Winters himself would lead the attack.

It was a dangerous mission, and Winters had only 12 men. But the German guns had to be silenced. Winters grabbed a rifle and went to scout out the cannons.

8:00 A.M.: Scoping Out the Enemy

Winters studied the enemy's position. The field was bordered on all sides by high, thick bushes called hedgerows.

He could see that the Germans had hidden their cannons on the far side of the field, deep inside the hedgerows. The powerful 105-mm guns were aimed directly at Utah Beach.

U.S. soldiers fire from behind hedgerows as they battle Germans in Normandy. These high, thick hedges bordered many farm fields in the region.

A network of deep trenches connected the four gun positions. Winters figured there were about 50 enemy soldiers in the trenches—artillerymen manning the cannons, and infantrymen defending them.

Winters knew he was in a tough spot. His men were outnumbered four to one. And they'd be attacking the most difficult kind of target—a well-entrenched position. The deep trenches provided excellent protection for the Germans. As long as they stayed low, it would be difficult to kill them.

But Winters did have one advantage—the element of surprise.

And he had a plan. It would require daring, speed, and teamwork. But Easy Company was one of the best-trained units in the U.S. Army.

They were ready.

8:30 A.M.: Into the Trenches

Winters gathered his men and gave them their orders.

They'd be attacking from the enemy's rear and from the sides. They would take out the nearest gun first, and then the others.

Winters broke the squad into groups. He placed two machine guns in hedgerows about 100 yards behind the cannons. They would provide covering fire to keep the enemy pinned down while Winters and others advanced on the trenches.

Then he ordered two riflemen to sneak up closer and hide to the side of the guns, behind some trees. From there, they could try to pick off Germans in the trenches.

At Winters's signal, the two machine guns opened fire, surprising the enemy. Some Germans rushed to fire back, but many stayed low in the trenches, taking cover from the machine-gun fire.

Two soldiers from Easy Company man a machine gun in Normandy.

With the Germans distracted, a group led by Lt. Buck Compton began to creep across the field toward the first cannon. Soon, the men were close enough to rush the nearest trench.

With the riflemen and machine gunners still providing covering fire, Compton raced forward, hurling grenades as he ran. Winters and three other men were right behind him.

U.S. troops keep low as they advance through enemy-held territory.

U.S. infantrymen attack a well-defended German position.

They reached the trench and jumped in, their guns blasting. The German soldiers took off down the trench. One threw a "potato-masher" grenade as he retreated. Winters yelled out a warning, and the men scattered before it exploded.

Still throwing grenades, the Americans chased the Germans through the trenches. Winters shot and killed three of them, and his men hit several others. Then he spotted two Germans turning their machine gun toward his squad. He shot them before they could fire.

Easy Company had captured the first cannon.

Over the next few hours, Winters and his men, with the help of reinforcements, battled in the trenches to capture the other

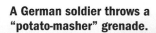

A German soldier throws a "potato-masher" grenade.

three guns. During the fierce close-up fighting, 15 Germans and four Americans were killed. And Easy Company took 12 prisoners.

By the afternoon of D-Day, Allied soldiers and supplies were landing safely on the Normandy beaches.

By noon, the guns at Brécourt Manor had been silenced. And on Utah Beach, the troops were landing safely.

12 noon: Mission Accomplished

On D-Day, about 23,000 U.S. soldiers came ashore at Utah Beach. There were fewer casualties than expected.

The troops, along with tanks and other vehicles, were able to make their way inland on the four exit roads secured by Easy Company and other paratroopers from the 101st Airborne.

But the paratroopers paid a high price for the success of their mission. Of the 6,600 men in the 101st who jumped into Normandy on D-Day, 1,250 were killed, wounded, or taken prisoner.

As Lieutenant Dick Winters fell asleep that night, he could hear shooting nearby. He knew there was lots of hard fighting ahead. But for now, he was just relieved to have survived his first day of combat.

3

Wounded American soldiers take shelter
behind a wall on Omaha Beach. Many of their
comrades were cut down by German machine
guns as soon as they landed.

U.S. troops were being slaughtered on Omaha Beach. But as small groups of men took on the enemy, the tide of battle turned.

BLOODY OMAHA

A view from one of the 5,000 Allied ships on their way to Normandy. Most were from the British and U.S. navies.

The rough waters of the English Channel pounded the transport ships' steel hulls. Soldiers held tight to their guns and tried not to think about what awaited them at the end of their journey.

The men were part of the largest seaborne invasion force in the history of the world. They had left Britain the day before. Now it was early morning on June 6, 1944—D-Day.

Under a cloudy gray sky, 5,000 ships steamed toward France. They ranged in size from giant warships to small fishing boats.

The fleet included battleships and destroyers armed with massive guns. Transport ships were packed with the 150,000 ground troops who would storm the beaches of Normandy. Other vessels carried tanks, cannons, and equipment.

Every fighting man onboard knew his mission was nothing short of ending the war in Europe.

A late-night storm had kicked up six-foot-high waves. British cooks offered their soldiers a feast—steak and eggs, pork chops, ice cream. But most were too seasick to eat. Instead, they cleaned their weapons and scribbled letters home.

Two Coast Guardsmen man their gun on the way to Normandy.

"There weren't many men who got much sleep," Lt. Col. Alfred Birra wrote to his wife. "For the most part, we sat around, talked, played cards, drank coffee, and did the usual things a man does when he is worried and a little scared and doesn't want to show it."

The lead ships carried the first waves of soldiers. They would go ashore at dawn. Some were from the U.S. Army's 1st and 29th divisions. Their target was a vital stretch of coastline codenamed Omaha Beach.

Their job was to clear the way for the troops landing behind them. But to capture Omaha Beach,

A few days before D-Day, soldiers study a model of Omaha Beach to prepare for the dangerous mission ahead.

they would have to attack and destroy the well-fortified German defenses along the six-mile beach.

The troops were nervous, but they had high hopes for success. The invasion plan called for warships to bombard the beach before the troops landed. And amphibious tanks—which could move through water—would land just ahead of the troops. They'd take out any remaining German cannons and machine guns.

Chuck Hurlbut, a 19-year-old from New York, thought the invasion would go off like clockwork. "This is gonna be easy," Hurlbut thought.

But nothing about D-Day would be easy. The Germans believed the invasion force would land near Calais, but they hadn't left Normandy undefended. And some of Hitler's best troops had been assigned to defend Omaha Beach. They had turned it into a heavily armed fortress.

The enemy was preparing a slaughter on the beach.

"We Were Cut to Pieces"

Hours before dawn, loudspeakers blared over the ships' decks. It was time to go.

In the darkness, the first wave of 1,500 soldiers climbed over the hulls of the transport ships. They lowered themselves down rope ladders into landing craft, small wooden boats that carried up to 36 soldiers each.

At 4:30 A.M., the landing craft began their 11-mile trip to shore. The flat-bottomed boats were tossed by the roaring waves. Water crashed over the sides. The men were soaked and seasick. Seawater mixed with vomit rose around their feet.

"It was a terrible ride into the beach," said mortar expert Bob Slaughter. "A tremendous [wave] swamped our boat. The water would come over the sides and just soak us and make our seasickness worse."

Soon, Allied battleships opened fire on the beaches. Hurlbut's ears rang from the deafening explosions. Thousands of shells screamed across the sky. "How in the world can anyone

U.S. soldiers packed into a landing craft head toward the coast of Normandy.

Artillery guns on a U.S. battleship
pound the coast of France.

survive what [the Germans are] receiving?" he thought. "There's
going to be nobody alive when we get there."

Three miles from shore, the invasion plan hit its first deadly
snag. The amphibious tanks rolled off their transport ships and
headed for shore. But the high waves tore through their floats.
Most of the tanks, along with their crews, sank to the bottom of
the channel.

Some of the landing craft also capsized. Drowning soldiers,
weighed down with equipment, cried for help. But the captains
of the landing craft were under strict orders: Stop for no one!

"The guys started bobbing up to the surface, floating like
corks, screaming and yelling," Hurlbut recalled. "We just went
right by them. Right then I saw that compassion is not a part
of war. You've got a mission to do; nothing can interrupt it."

As the boats approached the beach, the troops heard
only silence. Omaha was covered in clouds of dust. Maybe,
soldiers prayed, the early-morning shelling had done the
trick. Maybe the enemy's defenses had been destroyed and
its soldiers killed.

Suddenly, the beach erupted with German machine-gun fire. Soldiers heard the pinging of bullets against the metal ramps of their boats. Then artillery shells screamed overhead and exploded among the landing craft.

Now, 100 yards from shore, the landing craft lowered their ramps—and soldiers plunged into neck-deep water. Many were instantly torn apart by German gunfire. The dying and wounded fell into the waves. The surf ran red with blood.

"The ramp went down and [our captain] was the first man off, and they just riddled him," said Private Robert Sales, a radio operator. "Everybody who went off, [the Germans] just cut them down. We were cut to pieces."

Of the 30 men in his landing craft, Sales was the only survivor.

A German soldier mans a machine gun high above a beach in Nazi-occupied France.

On D-Day, war photographer Robert Capa captured the first moments of the landing on Omaha Beach. This photo shows troops behind steel obstacles, trying to take cover from German gunfire.

Bloody Omaha

Troops stumbled through the surf, past the dead bodies of their fellow soldiers.

They crawled onto the beach, their hearts pounding. The screams and cries of wounded and dying men filled the air.

Ahead of the soldiers lay 200 yards of open beach. The Germans had covered it with mines and barbed wire. They had also planted jagged piles of steel beams in the sand. These and other obstacles were designed to tear apart any boats that tried to approach at high tide.

A rocky embankment ran along the high-tide line near the top of the beach. If the men could reach the embankment, it might provide some cover. But first, they would have to cross the beach while under constant fire from cannons and machine guns positioned in the bluffs beyond the beach.

The invasion was just minutes old, and already it seemed like a disaster. The few tanks that made it to shore had been blown up. Hundreds of wounded and dead Americans lay on the bloody

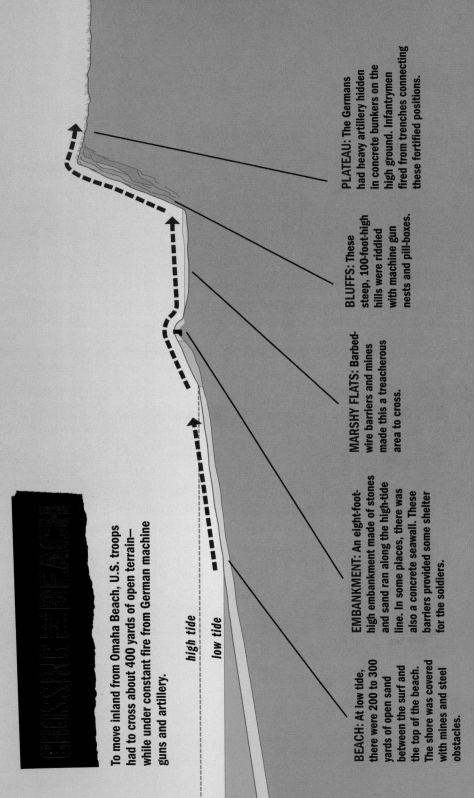

CROSSING THE BEACH

To move inland from Omaha Beach, U.S. troops had to cross about 400 yards of open terrain—while under constant fire from German machine guns and artillery.

high tide

low tide

BEACH: At low tide, there were 200 to 300 yards of open sand between the surf and the top of the beach. The shore was covered with mines and steel obstacles.

EMBANKMENT: An eight-foot-high embankment made of stones and sand ran along the high-tide line. In some places, there was also a concrete seawall. These barriers provided some shelter for the soldiers.

MARSHY FLATS: Barbed-wire barriers and mines made this a treacherous area to cross.

BLUFFS: These steep, 100-foot-high hills were riddled with machine gun nests and pill-boxes.

PLATEAU: The Germans had heavy artillery hidden in concrete bunkers on the high ground. Infantrymen fired from trenches connecting these fortified positions.

Under heavy fire from German guns, troops try to cross the open beach.

sand. Survivors hid beneath dead bodies. No one dared to move forward.

"All I could see was chaos, catastrophe," Hurlbut recalled. "Boats burning, smoking, dead men all along the water's edge, dead bodies. . . . It was awful, awful, awful. . . . I laid there and I just cried like a baby for a while."

Pinned Down

The soldiers knew they'd never survive if they stayed at the water's edge. They began inching their way forward.

Some men took cover behind the steel obstacles, but many were cut down as they advanced. Still, despite the relentless enemy fire, some soldiers managed to reach the wall near the top of the beach.

The eight-foot-high embankment provided a bit of shelter. Troops huddled there in shell-shocked groups. Some cried. Others stared vacantly ahead. Medics tried to help the wounded.

Now the Germans began lobbing mortar shells at the

On D-Day, medics braved enemy fire to tend to wounded soldiers on the beach.

embankment. The troops knew they couldn't stay there. But they were terrified, and there were few officers left to lead them.

Slowly, some men began organizing soldiers to move forward. One of them was Captain Joe Dawson. He knew that staying on the beach would be suicidal. It was only a matter of time before a German mortar found its mark.

"There was nothing I could do on the beach except die," Dawson said later.

Beyond the embankment lay a marshy area covered with deadly mines. Dawson's squad would have to cross the minefield—while under heavy fire. But first, they had to get past a barbed-wire barrier.

Two of Dawson's men snaked a bangalore torpedo—a long tube with an explosive at the end—over the top of the embankment. When it reached the barbed wire, they set off the explosive, blowing a gap in the wire.

They climbed over the wall and set off across the minefield, dodging bullets by rushing from one patch of brush to another. They reached the bluffs safely and began working their way to the high ground. Nearby, a squad led by Lieutenant John Spalding had also reached the base of the bluffs.

UP THE BLUFFS

Spalding knew that there were mines everywhere. But he figured there had to be a safe trail up the bluffs that the Germans used to travel between the beach and the high ground.

Two soldiers hurried ahead to look. When they sighted a narrow trail through a gully, Spalding didn't hesitate. "We're going up!" he yelled.

As Spalding and his men inched their way up the path, machine gunners high in the bluffs tried to pick them off. Several soldiers were hit, but the squad kept going, returning fire and hurling grenades as they advanced.

Suddenly, to their side, another machine gun opened fire. The men rushed the gunner and took him prisoner.

Then, in close fighting near the crest of the bluffs, Spalding's squad silenced several more guns and took more prisoners. They had succeeded in taking out the German defenses in that area.

Finally, they reached the top of the bluffs. Miraculously, no one had been critically injured on the way up. As Spalding said later, "We had an angel on each shoulder on that trip."

Spalding's squad took this path up the bluffs. By the time this photo was taken, engineers had marked the trail and removed mines in the area.

Spalding lit a yellow smoke flare to signal that they had broken through. On the beach below, soldiers began heading toward the smoke.

Dawson's squad and a few others had also fought their way up the bluffs. The seemingly impenetrable Nazi stronghold was beginning to crack. It was 11:00 A.M. And suddenly there was a glimmer of hope.

Securing the Beaches

As the yellow smoke from Spalding's flare wafted over the beach, the tide of the battle began to turn.

On other parts of the beach, small units began moving up the bluffs, using flamethrowers and grenades to flush the enemy out of their bunkers and strongpoints. Gradually, they eliminated

The day after D-Day. U.S. troops make their way up the bluffs from Omaha Beach.

the gunners who had terrorized the landing force.

By 1:30 P.M, U.S. troops were on their way to controlling Omaha Beach. Soon, men and equipment were safely moving inland. It had taken 34,000 American troops to secure this vital beachhead—at a cost of 2,500 dead or wounded soldiers.

The Allied victory on the Normandy beaches marked the beginning of the end for the Nazis. Within three months, two million Allied troops had landed and were fighting their way across France, headed for Germany.

General Dwight Eisenhower recognized the dedication and bravery of the men who fought on D-Day. "I asked [them] to die for freedom and they were ready to do it," he said later, "and that's why they are heroes."

For his actions on D-Day, John Spalding was awarded the Distinguished Service Cross by General Eisenhower.

British and Canadian soldiers take cover behind a dune. Troops from Britain and Canada captured three of the five Normandy beaches on D-Day.

EUROPE LIBERATED

Operation Overlord was one of the largest military offensives in history. Within three months, two million U.S., British, and Canadian soldiers had fanned out across Nazi-held France, headed for the heart of Germany. But the Germans fought back fiercely, and the Allies lost a quarter of a million troops during their push through France.

On August 25, 1944, Allied tanks rolled into Paris. After four years of Nazi rule, France was free once again.

In a radio address on New Year's Day in 1945, Hitler declared that "Germany will never capitulate." But by then, ten million Allied soldiers were closing in on all sides. And Allied bombers were raining destruction on German cities.

U.S. troops surround a farmhouse in France, searching for a German sniper.

In March, U.S. and British armies pushed across Germany's western border. And the Soviet Red Army closed in from the east.

U.S. troops in Paris on August 29, 1944

"I Have No Words"

As the troops fought their way through Germany, they uncovered horrors that left even the most hardened veterans speechless. Behind the barbed-wire fences of Buchenwald, Dachau, and other German concentration camps, they found stark evidence of the crime the world would come to call the Holocaust.

Human bodies lay in heaps. There were gas chambers disguised as shower rooms; ovens for incinerating the corpses; piles of the victims' shoes. Twelve million people had died in Hitler's camps, including six million Jews. The survivors were little more than walking skeletons.

Survivors found by U.S. troops who liberated the Buchenwald concentration camp on April 11, 1945

In a radio report from Buchenwald, reporter Edward R. Murrow told his radio listeners, "I reported what I saw and heard, but only part of it. For most of it, I have no words."

Germany surrendered to the Allies on May 7, 1945. The war against Japan ended three months later, after the U.S. dropped atomic bombs on the cities of Hiroshima and Nagasaki. World War II was over.

D-Day had been the turning point of the war. On June 6, 2009, the 65th anniversary of D-Day, President Barack Obama paid tribute to the Allied soldiers who fought on the beaches of Normandy. "The bravery and selflessness of a few," he said, "was able to change the course of an entire century."

TIMELINE

JANUARY 1933: Adolf Hitler becomes chancellor of Germany.

SEPTEMBER 1935: Germany issues anti-Semitic laws stripping Jews of their citizenship and rights.

MARCH 1938: Germany takes over Austria.

MARCH 1939: Germany invades Czechoslovakia, breaking its promises to Britain and France.

AUGUST 1939: Germany and the USSR sign an agreement not to attack each other.

SEPTEMBER 1939: Germany invades Poland. In response, France and Britain declare war on Germany, and World War II begins.

APRIL–MAY 1940: Germany invades Denmark, Norway, France, Belgium, Luxembourg, and the Netherlands.

JUNE 1940: Germany captures Paris. Eight days later, France surrenders to Germany.

SEPTEMBER 1940: Germany, Italy, and Japan form an alliance known as the Axis. Germany begins bombing London and other British cities. The attacks would continue until the end of the war, killing more than 60,000 people.

JUNE 1941: Germany invades the USSR, breaking their non-aggression agreement.

DECEMBER 7, 1941: Japan attacks the U.S. Pacific Fleet based at Pearl Harbor, Hawaii. The next day, the U.S. declares war on Japan. In response, Hitler declares war on the U.S.

NOVEMBER 1942: The Allies attack and eventually defeat Axis forces in North Africa.

SEPTEMBER 1943: Italy surrenders to the Allies.

JUNE 6, 1944: D-Day. The Allies land on the beaches of Normandy, France. It is the first step in the liberation of Western Europe.

APRIL 30, 1945: With the Soviet Red Army advancing through Berlin, Adolf Hitler commits suicide.

MAY 7, 1945: Germany surrenders, ending the war in Europe.

AUGUST 6, 1945: The United States drops an atomic bomb that destroys the Japanese city of Hiroshima. Three days later, the U.S. drops another atomic bomb on the city of Nagasaki.

AUGUST 14, 1945: Japan surrenders. World War II ends.

RESOURCES

BOOKS

Adams, Simon. *World War II (DK Eyewitness Books).* New York: DK Publishing, 2007.

Ambrose, Stephen E. *The Good Fight: How World War II Was Won.* New York: Atheneum, 2001.

Anderson, Christopher J. *Screaming Eagles: The 101st Airborne Division from D-Day to Desert Storm.* Philadelphia: Chelsea House, 2002.

Birkner, Michael J. *Dwight D. Eisenhower: America's 34th President (Encyclopedia of Presidents, Second Series).* New York: Children's Press, 2005.

Brook, Henry. *True Stories of D-Day.* New York: Scholastic Inc., 2006.

Drez, Ronald J. *Remember D-Day: The Plan, the Invasion, Survivor Stories.* Washington, D.C.: National Geographic Books, 2004.

Nicholson, Makanaonalani Dorinda. *Remember World War II: Kids Who Survived Tell Their Stories.* Washington, D.C.: National Geographic Books, 2005.

Wallace, Karen. *D-Day Landings: The Story of the Allied Invasion.* New York: DK Publishing, 2004.

WEBSITES

D-Day (American Experience)
www.pbs.org/wgbh/amex/dday
The online companion to *D-Day*, an episode from the acclaimed PBS series *American Experience.*

D-Day: June 6, 1944
www.army.mil/d-day
The U.S. Army's official D-Day website includes photographs, maps, and information about the divisions that took part in the Normandy campaign.

The D-Day Museum
www.ddaymuseum.co.uk
The website of the D-Day Museum in Portsmouth, England.

The National World War II Museum
www.nationalww2museum.org
The National World War II Museum explores U.S. involvement in World War II through personal accounts, artifacts, photographs, and film footage.

Voices of D-Day
www.bbc.co.uk/history/worldwars/ wwtwo/dday_audio.shtml
Hear the stories of eight people who experienced D-Day firsthand.

DICTIONARY

A

alliance (uh-LYE-uhnss) *noun* an agreement to join forces and work together

Allies (AL-eyes) *noun* the alliance of nations that fought against the Axis powers during World War II; the three major Allied powers were the United States, Great Britain, and the Soviet Union

amphibious tank (am-FIB-ee-uhs TANK) *noun* a tank that can move through water

anti-aircraft fire (AN-tee AIR-kraft FIRE) *noun* gunfire aimed at enemy planes

anti-Semitic (AN-tee seh-MIT-ik) *adjective* prejudiced or hostile toward Jews

anti-tank mine (AN-tee TANK MINE) *noun* an explosive device placed in the ground and designed to damage tanks and other vehicles

artillery (ar-TIL-uh-ree) *noun* large, crew-operated guns such as cannons and mortars

Axis (AK-siss) *noun* the alliance of nations opposed to the Allies during World War II; the three major Axis powers were Germany, Italy, and Japan

B

blitzkrieg (BLITZ-kreeg) *noun* German term for an intense military campaign intended to bring about a swift victory; *blitzkrieg* means "lightning war"

D

D-Day (DEE DAY) *noun* a day set for launching a military operation; specifically, the date of the Allied landing in northern France during World War II (June 6, 1944)

democracy (di-MOK-ruh-see) *noun* a system of government in which the people choose their leaders in free elections

dictator (DIK-tay-tur) *noun* a leader who has total authority over a country, often ruling through intimidation or force

drop zone (DROP ZOHN) *noun* a designated area into which troops or supplies are dropped by parachute

G

garrison (GA-ruh-suhn) *noun* a group of soldiers whose assignment is to guard a particular town or fort

GI (jee-EYE) *noun* slang for an American soldier

grenade (gruh-NADE) *noun* a small bomb thrown by hand or fired from a rifle

I

infantry (IN-fuhn-tree) *noun* the part of an army that fights on foot

L

landing craft (LAND-ing KRAFT) *noun* a boat designed for moving troops and equipment from a transport ship to a beach during a military assault

M

mortar (MOR-tur) *noun* a short, lightweight cannon that fires shells or rockets high in the air

P

paratrooper (PA-ruh-troop-uhr) *noun* a soldier who is trained to jump by parachute into battle

potato masher (puh-TAY-toh MASH-uhr) *noun* British slang term for the standard, sticklike hand grenade of the German army during World War II

T

tracer bullet (TRAY-suhr BUL-it) *noun* a bullet whose course is made visible in flight by a trail of flames or smoke, used to assist gunners in aiming in the dark

transport ship (TRANSS-port SHIP) *noun* a ship for carrying soldiers or military equipment

INDEX

ABOUT THIS BOOK

D-Day was a major turning point in modern world history, and many fine books have been written about the events of June 6, 1944. The story of the Allied invasion of Normandy has also been powerfully dramatized in several movies and TV series.

The following books and websites were very helpful while writing this book.

BOOKS

Ambrose, Stephen E. *Band of Brothers: E Company, 506th Regiment, 101st Airborne from Normandy to Hitler's Eagle's Nest.* New York: Simon & Schuster, 1992.

Ambrose, Stephen E. *D-Day, June 6, 1944: The Climactic Battle of World War II.* New York: Simon & Schuster, 1994.

Balkoski, Joseph. *Omaha Beach: D-Day, June 6, 1944.* Mechanicsburg, PA: Stackpole Books, 2004.

Bliven Jr., Bruce. *The Story of D-Day: June 6, 1944.* New York: Random House, 1956.

Botting, Douglas. *The Second Front.* New York: Time-Life Books, 1978.

Cross, Robin, Messenger, Charles, and H. P. Willmott. *World War II.* New York: DK Publishing, 2004.

Major Winters, Dick, with Colonel Cole C. Kingseed. *Beyond Band of Brothers: The War Memoirs of Major Dick Winters.* New York: Berkley Caliber, 2006.

Ryan, Cornelius. *The Longest Day.* New York: Simon & Schuster, 1959.

Yarrington, Gary A., ed. *World War II: Personal Accounts Pearl Harbor to V-J Day.* Austin, TX: Lyndon Baines Johnson Foundation, 1992.

WEBSITES

www.ddaymuseum.org
www.army.mil/d-day
www.warchronicle.com/dday/contents.htm
www.skylighters.org/photos/robertcapa.html
www.pbs.org/wgbh/amex/dday
www.militaryhistoryonline.com/wwii/dday
      Benjamin Alvarado Collection (AFC/2001/001/32448), Veterans History Project, American Folklife Center, Library of Congress